THIS WALKER BOOK BELONGS TO:

_____

_____

_____

WELCOME TO THE VIKING WORLD.
I AM MUNINN, BIRD OF MEMORY.
I SEE ALL THINGS, AND NEVER
FORGET THEM. I SAW THE SAGA
OF HARRI BRISTLEBEARD AS IT
HAPPENED, AND NOW I WILL TELL
IT TO YOU. IT IS THE STORY OF
FOUR GREAT HEROES AND THEIR
ADVENTURES IN THE FAR AND
FEARFUL NORTH. LET
ME INTRODUCE
YOU TO THEM.

First published 1997
by Walker Books Ltd
87 Vauxhall Walk, London SE11 5HJ

This edition published 2006

2 4 6 8 10 9 7 5 3 1

Text © 1997 Jonathan Stroud   Illustrations © 1997 Cathy Gale

The right of Jonathan Stroud and Cathy Gale to be identified as
author and illustrator respectively of this work has been asserted by
them in accordance with the Copyright, Designs and Patents Act 1988

This book has been typeset in Lithos and Highlander

Printed in China

All rights reserved

British Library Cataloguing in Publication Data:
a catalogue record for this book is available from the British Library

ISBN-13: 978-1-84428-768-0   ISBN-10: 1-84428-768-8

www.walkerbooks.co.uk

WALKER BOOKS
AND SUBSIDIARIES
LONDON · BOSTON · SYDNEY · AUCKLAND

**HAROLD BRISTLEBEARD, known**
as Harri. A hairy Norseman. He wants
to win fame and fortune for his village.

**GUNNHILD FINEHAIR,**
known as Hilda. A master
archer and a little bored of
things at home. Fenrir the
Wolf's best friend.

**WILFRID,** an English slave. Keeps
Harri well fed and in a good temper.

# THE VIKING SAGA OF HARRI BRISTLEBEARD

## A HEROIC PUZZLE ADVENTURE

To Mum and Dad
J.S.

To Dad and Mum
C.G.

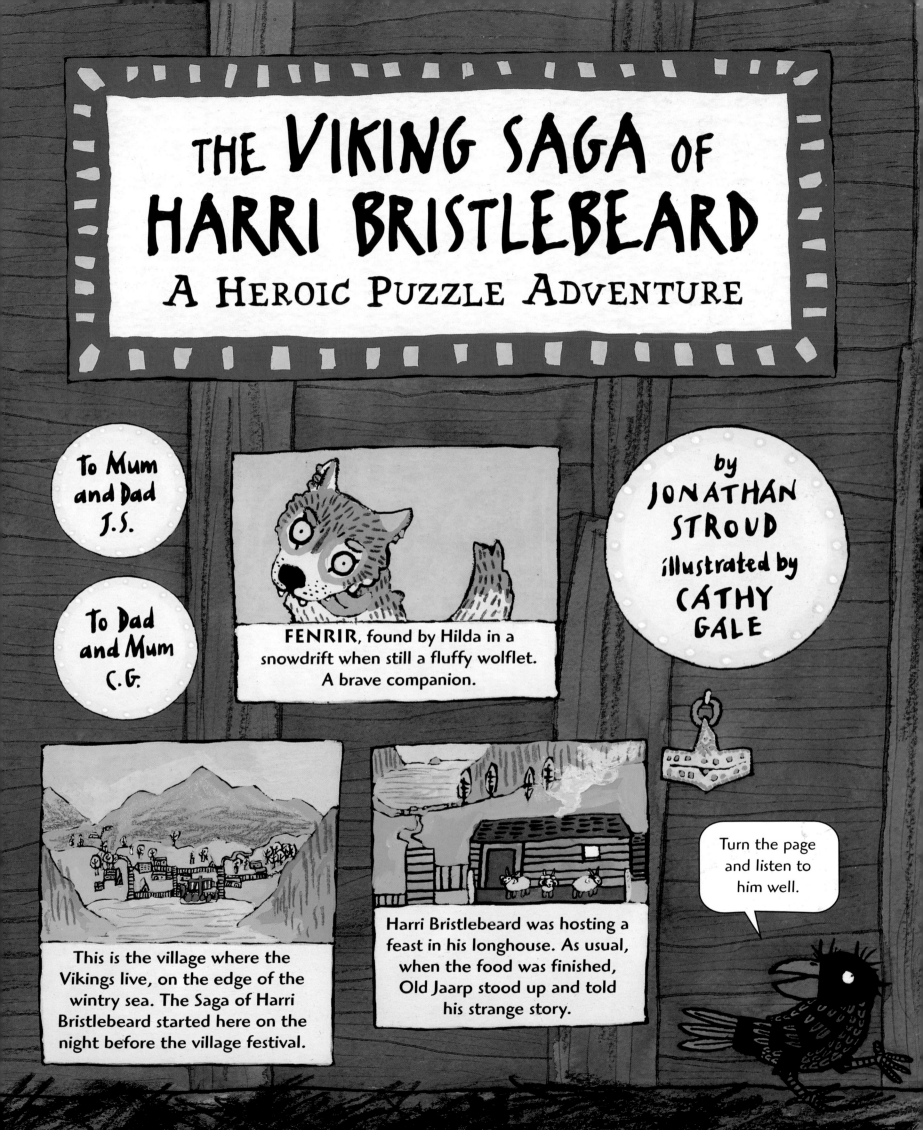

FENRIR, found by Hilda in a snowdrift when still a fluffy wolflet. A brave companion.

by JONATHAN STROUD

illustrated by CATHY GALE

This is the village where the Vikings live, on the edge of the wintry sea. The Saga of Harri Bristlebeard started here on the night before the village festival.

Harri Bristlebeard was hosting a feast in his longhouse. As usual, when the food was finished, Old Jaarp stood up and told his strange story.

Turn the page and listen to him well.

Many years ago, Magnus Ironjaw was our chief, and he carried a magic raven banner.

The banner brought us luck. Magnus never lost a battle. Even the wicked world serpent fled when it saw us come sailing.

But one day disaster struck. A dragon came from the sky, snatched the banner and flew away with it.

Magnus and his men leapt into his ship, the Golden Cockerel, and set off in pursuit.

They were never seen again, our luck has ended and the village has grown poor.

But every year, during the festival, we set sail and search for the missing raven banner, which will bring luck back to us all.

Vikings love riddles and other puzzles, and like a true Viking you must solve the puzzles I set you as I tell the Saga.

 For a start, look out for me. In every scene I am magically disguised, but always keep a raven's shape.
**Can you see me here?**

 Bjorn, the longhouse lemming, has been driven out of his home.
**Can you see him?**

 Hilda planned to sail with Harri. She decided to notice landmarks that would help find the way home. Her first was the yellow weathercock.
**Can you see it?**

## No, no.
It's far too dangerous for a girl.

Uncle Harri, may I sail with you tomorrow?

I'll take my food bag with me on the voyage.

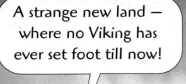

"A strange new land — where no Viking has ever set foot till now!"

"Erm, I wouldn't be too sure about that. Look!"

All around were shipwrecks locked in the ice. Nothing moved, but I was watching. **Can you see me?**

Three Northern lemmings came to join the company. **Can you see all nine?**

Hilda's landmark here was a giant arch of sea-ice. **Where was it?**

"Look what Fenrir's found. Magnus has left a message!"

THE ICE HAS TRAPPED OUR SHIP. THE DRAGON FLEW OVER THE MOUNTAINS WITH THE BANNER. WE TRIED TO FOLLOW, BUT TROLLS DROVE US BACK. WE HAVE LOST THE BANNER, BUT MY HIDDEN RUNE ᚴ SHOWS THE WAY TO ANYONE BRAVE ENOUGH TO SEEK IT.

MAGNUS

*Which way did they have to go to follow the dragon's trail?*

THE VIKINGS WERE DETERMINED TO FOLLOW THE TRAIL OF THE RAVEN BANNER AND SEARCHED THE AREA CAREFULLY. FIRST THEY FOUND THE GOLDEN COCKEREL, WHICH HAD BEEN SPLIT IN TWO BY THE ICE. THEN THEY FOUND MAGNUS'S RUNE ON A BROKEN MAST BESIDE A PATH AND SET OFF INTO THE MOUNTAINS.

Er, Mr Bristlebeard, aren't you worried about the trolls?

Not at all!

Mr Bristlebeard, what would you do if you met a troll?

Hold on, Fenrir, I'll save you!

EEEOOOOOW!

Grrrrr – SNAP!

*Which stick did Hilda have to shoot away with her arrow to make a boulder fall on the troll's head?*

HILDA'S ARROW HIT THE GREEN STICK AND THE BOULDER STRUCK THE TROLL'S HEAD. BUT IT WAS ALL IN VAIN. THE VIKINGS WERE CAPTURED AND TAKEN TO THE TROLLS' CASTLE. THE OTHERS WERE CHAINED UP IN SEPARATE CELLS, BUT WILFRID, ARMED WITH THE BLUE TOADSTOOL, ASKED TO SEE THE KING.

It's no use trying to plead. You're the first course.

Serves you right.

It is a great honor to be eaten by you, O King. For starters, may I recommend my mushroom surprise?

Don't mind if I do.

I like a challenge!

Stop him!

Wilfrid first had to find the castle key so he could unlock his friends' chains. He could not go into any room with a troll in it. *How could he get to the key?* Then he had to collect their weapons before rescuing Fenrir, Hilda, and Harri (in that order) and finding a way out. *Can you trace Wilfrid's route through the castle?*

FENRIR'S PARENTS WERE THE WOLVES STANDING UNDER A TREE WITH AN OWL IN IT. THEY AGREED TO ESCORT THE VIKINGS THROUGH THE FOREST. PAST THE ENORMOUS FOOTPRINT THEY WENT, TOWARDS THE DRAGON-GLOW ON THE HORIZON.

This is good luck for us!

It's getting a trifle warm.

You are in the realm of Ragnar Crispy. To all those who come, I ask a riddle. If you cannot answer, I will eat you.

While you are thinking, you should chew the leaves of the fire-proof plant, or you will roast before I get to taste you.

I'll solve the riddle.

RAGNAR CRISPY'S RIDDLE

WE ARE MADE OF WOOD AND IRON,
SCARRED BY SWORDS IN HEAT OF BATTLE.
OUR SHAPES ARE THE SAME,
BUT NOT OUR COLOURS:
ONE RED, ONE GREEN, ONE BLUE;
THINK HARD;
CAN YOU TELL US OUR NAME?

WILFRID SOON FOUND THE FIRE-PROOF PLANT SHELTERING BETWEEN TWO HELMETS. THEY ALL TOOK A LEAF, BUT HILDA WAS STILL THINKING, AND TIME WAS RUNNING OUT!

I've got it! The answer is SHIELDS! Look! There are three shields here!

You're the first who's ever got it right.

Well, it was a very clever riddle.

Many years ago four of the five carved stones from my necklace were stolen and scattered across the North. Have you seen them on your travels? If so, I will do you a favour in return.

Look at all those banners on the wall!

One of them must be the magic Raven Banner.

Which was the Raven Banner? Think back to Old Jaarp's tale.

WILFRID HAD SEEN THE STONES – ONE IN THE FOREST, ONE IN THE MOUNTAINS, ONE AMONG THE SHIPWRECKS AND ONE ON THE OUTSKIRTS OF THEIR VILLAGE! MEANWHILE, HARRI HAD SEEN THE RAVEN BANNER NEXT TO THE GOLDEN AXE. IT WAS TIME TO DO SOME BARGAINING.

So that's where my stones are! Thank you! Ask any favour you like!

Could you help us get home please?

I'll fly you back myself.

You'll have to direct me. We'll pick up my stones on the way.

At last, I can use my landmarks!

First find the dragon's chimney far down below them. Then, using Hilda's landmarks, retrace their journey over land and sea until you reach their home.

ACROSS THE WORLD THEY FLEW, UNTIL AT LAST THE DRAGON SET THEM DOWN IN THEIR VILLAGE ONCE AGAIN. HE COLLECTED THE FINAL STONE FOR HIS NECKLACE AND SET OFF INTO THE SKY.

Goodbye! Thanks for the trousers.

**Help!** The dragon! He'll eat us all!

All right, don't panic. We're back, and we've brought the banner. But before I show it to you, would someone please bring me a new pair of trousers?

What are you going to do next, Hilda?

I'm going to build a ship of my own and see the world.

Harri had hung the banner up in pride of place, but there were four other changes to his wall since the last feast.
*Can you spot them?*

Wilfrid, you have been a brave companion. You are a slave no longer.

Thank you, Mr Bristlebeard. I'll make a freedom feast to celebrate.

As the Viking heroes gathered round the table, I was watching still. *Can you see me?*

Bjorn the lemming arrived home with his 21 friends. *Now who was told to leave?*

Hey! Who's been nibbling this?

Wilfrid was holding a tasty honey cake, but someone had already sneaked a bite.
*Can you guess who it was?*

THAT IS THE END OF THE SAGA. I SAW WHAT HAPPENED NEXT.

HARRI BECAME A GREAT VIKING LEADER. WITH THE RAVEN BANNER BESIDE HIM, HE NEVER LOST A BATTLE.

HILDA BECAME A FAMOUS VIKING EXPLORER. FENRIR BECAME THE VERY FIRST WOLF TO SAIL RIGHT ROUND THE WORLD.

WILFRID BECAME A GREAT CHEF. ONE DAY HE RETURNED TO ENGLAND AND COOKED FOR KING ALFRED.

I SAW ALL THESE THINGS. BUT THEY ARE OTHER STORIES, AND THIS ONE IS AT AN END.

WALKER BOOKS is the world's leading

independent publisher of children's books.

Working with the best authors and illustrators

we create books for all ages, from babies

to teenagers – books your child will

grow up with and always remember. So…

FOR THE BEST CHILDREN'S BOOKS,
LOOK FOR THE BEAR